Loving Someone with Bipolar Disorder

A Guide to Understanding and Supporting Your Partner with Bipolar Disorder

Cynthia Jackson D.A

Table of Contents

Love is the light that shines even in the darkest moments of bipolar disorder."

DEDICATION

Dedicated to all the partners, family members, and friends who love someone with bipolar disorder. Your support, understanding, and unwavering love are invaluable to those who are navigating the ups and downs of this illness. May this book provide you with the knowledge, tools, and inspiration to continue on this journey together, with hope and resilience.

MOTIVATION FROM JENNY AND TOM

Jenny and Tom had been together for three years, and things were going great. They had their ups and downs like any couple, but they were always able to work through them. Tom was diagnosed with bipolar disorder two years ago, and although it was a shock to both of them, they were committed to working through it together.

Jenny knew that Tom's mood swings could be unpredictable and sometimes challenging to handle. But she also knew that Tom was more than his disorder, and she loved him for who he was, not just for his diagnosis.

One day, Tom had a severe depressive episode that lasted for weeks. He was distant, uncommunicative, and didn't want to do anything. Jenny tried her best to be there for him, but it was hard not to take his behavior personally. She felt like he didn't care about her anymore and started to question their relationship.

But Jenny didn't give up on Tom or their relationship. She knew that bipolar disorder could be tough, but she also knew that Tom was worth fighting for. She reached out to Tom's therapist, educated herself about bipolar disorder, and joined a support group for loved ones of people with bipolar disorder.

Slowly but surely, Tom started to come out of his depressive episode with the help of his treatment and Jenny's unwavering support. They worked together to create a plan for future episodes, and Jenny learned how to take care of herself and set healthy boundaries.

Today, Jenny and Tom are still together, and they are stronger than ever. They've learned how to navigate the ups and downs of bipolar disorder together and have created a deep understanding and love for each other.

INTRODUCTION

Loving someone with bipolar disorder can be a challenging and emotionally exhausting journey. It can be difficult to understand the unpredictable mood swings, impulsive behaviors, and intense emotional episodes that come with this mental health condition. However, with the right tools and support, it is possible to build a strong and fulfilling relationship with your loved one.

This book is a comprehensive guide for anyone who is in a relationship with someone who has bipolar disorder. It provides practical strategies and advice for navigating the ups and downs of the illness, as well as tips for maintaining a healthy and fulfilling relationship. Whether you are a partner, family member, or friend, this book will help you better understand the challenges and opportunities of loving someone with bipolar disorder.

Throughout this book, we will explore the symptoms and causes of bipolar disorder, the importance of seeking professional treatment, and the various treatment options available. We will also discuss how to communicate effectively, manage conflict, and develop a crisis plan to ensure your loved one's safety. Additionally, we will explore the impact of bipolar disorder on intimacy and offer strategies for maintaining a strong emotional connection.

Caring for yourself as a caregiver is also essential, and we will discuss the importance of self-care, setting boundaries, and managing expectations. Finally, we will provide resources and support for individuals with bipolar disorder and their loved ones.

This book is not only a guide for navigating the challenges of bipolar disorder but also a testament to the power of love and the importance of building a support network. With the right tools and support, you can build a fulfilling and loving relationship with your partner, despite the challenges of bipolar disorder.

Understanding Bipolar Disorder

Definition of mood disorder

A mood disorder, also known as an affective disorder, is a mental health condition characterized by significant and persistent changes in a person's emotional state or mood. These changes in mood can affect an individual's ability to function in daily life and can impact their relationships, work, and overall well-being. Mood disorders can manifest as periods of depression, mania, or a combination of both, and can vary in severity and frequency. Examples of mood disorders include major depressive disorder, **bipolar disorder**, persistent depressive disorder (dysthymia), and cyclothymic disorder.

Types of Mood Disorders

There are several types of mood disorders, each with its own distinct symptoms, causes, and treatment approaches. The most common types of mood disorders include:

1. Major Depressive Disorder: This is a mood disorder characterized by persistent feelings of sadness, hopelessness, and a loss of interest or pleasure in activities that were once enjoyable. Symptoms may also include changes in appetite, sleep, energy level, and concentration, as well as feelings of worthlessness or guilt.

2. Bipolar Disorder: This is a mood disorder characterized by alternating episodes of depression and mania. During manic episodes, individuals may experience elevated or irritable mood, grandiosity,

impulsivity, and a decreased need for sleep. Bipolar disorder is further classified into different types, depending on the pattern and severity of symptoms.

3. Persistent Depressive Disorder (Dysthymia): This is a mood disorder characterized by chronic, low-grade depression that lasts for at least two years. Symptoms may include feelings of hopelessness, low self-esteem, and a lack of energy or motivation.

4. Cyclothymic Disorder: This is a mood disorder characterized by alternating periods of hypomanic and depressive symptoms that are less severe than those seen in bipolar disorder.

5. Seasonal Affective Disorder: This is a type of depression that occurs during the winter months when there is less natural sunlight. Symptoms may include low energy, increased sleep, and changes in appetite.

Other less common types of mood disorders include premenstrual dysphoric disorder (PMDD) and disruptive mood dysregulation disorder (DMDD). It's important to note that individuals may experience symptoms that overlap with more than one type of mood disorder, and accurate diagnosis and treatment require a thorough evaluation by a mental health professional.

History Of Mood Disorder

The history of mood disorders can be traced back to ancient times when various cultures and civilizations recognized the existence of these conditions. For example, ancient Greek and Roman physicians wrote about melancholia, a term used to describe severe and prolonged sadness.

In the 19th century, the French psychiatrist Jean-Étienne Dominique Esquirol first used the term "affective disorder" to describe a group of mental health conditions that involved changes in mood. Later, in the early 20th century, German psychiatrist Emil Kraepelin distinguished between bipolar disorder and major depressive disorder, two of the most common types of mood disorders.

Throughout the 20th century, advances in neuroscience and psychology led to a better understanding of the biological and psychological underpinnings of mood disorders. The development of antidepressant and mood-stabilizing medications in the 1950s and 1960s revolutionized the treatment of mood disorders, allowing individuals to manage their symptoms more effectively.

Today, mood disorders continue to be a major focus of research and treatment in the field of mental health. Advances in technology, such as brain imaging and genetic testing, are shedding new light on the causes and mechanisms of these conditions and helping clinicians develop more personalized and effective treatments.

What Is Bipolar Disorder?

Bipolar disorder is a mental health condition that affects a person's mood, energy, activity level, and ability to function. People with bipolar disorder experience episodes of both mania (an elevated, irritable, or euphoric mood) and depression (a low, sad, or hopeless mood). These episodes can vary in intensity and frequency and can be disruptive to a person's daily life and relationships. Bipolar disorder is classified into several types, including bipolar I disorder, bipolar II disorder, and cyclothymic disorder, among others. The exact cause of the bipolar disorder is not fully understood, but it is believed to be a combination of genetic, environmental, and neurological factors. Treatment typically involves a combination of medication, therapy, and lifestyle changes.

Symptoms Of Bipolar Disorder

The symptoms of bipolar disorder can vary widely depending on the type and severity of the condition, as well as the individual experiencing it. Some common symptoms of bipolar disorder include:

1. **Mania:** Elevated or irritable mood, increased energy and activity level, decreased need for sleep, racing thoughts, reckless behavior, grandiosity, poor judgment, and increased interest in pleasurable activities.
2. **Hypomania:** Similar to mania but with less severe symptoms, such as increased energy and activity level, decreased need for sleep, and elevated mood.
3. **Depression:** Low mood, feelings of hopelessness or worthlessness, decreased energy and activity level, difficulty sleeping or oversleeping, changes in appetite, difficulty concentrating, and thoughts of suicide.
4. **Mixed episode**: Symptoms of both mania and depression occurring at the same time or rapidly alternating between the two.
5. **Psychotic symptoms**: In severe cases, people with bipolar disorder may experience delusions or hallucinations, which can be frightening and disruptive.

It's important to note that not everyone with bipolar disorder experiences all of these symptoms, and the symptoms can vary in severity and frequency over time. Additionally, symptoms can be triggered or exacerbated by stress, life events, or substance use. If you or someone you know is experiencing symptoms of bipolar disorder, it's important to seek professional help for an accurate diagnosis and appropriate treatment.

Causes of bipolar disorder

The exact causes of bipolar disorder are not yet fully understood, but it is believed to be a combination of genetic, environmental, and neurological factors. Some potential causes of bipolar disorder include:

1. **Genetics**: esearch has suggested that genetics may play a role in the development of bipolar disorder. Studies have shown that the condition tends to run in families, and that individuals with a first-degree relative (such as a parent or sibling) with bipolar disorder have a higher risk of developing the condition themselves.While no single gene has been identified as causing bipolar disorder, research has identified several genes that may contribute to the development of the condition. These genes are involved in a variety of functions in the brain, including neurotransmitter signaling, circadian rhythms, and the regulation of mood and behavior.It's important to note that genetics is just one of several factors that can contribute to the development of the bipolar disorder. Environmental factors, such as stress, trauma, and substance use, can also play a role in the onset and progression of the condition. Additionally, not everyone with a family history of bipolar disorder will develop the condition, and not

everyone with bipolar disorder has a family history of the condition.

2. **Brain chemistry**: Bipolar disorder is also thought to be related to imbalances in certain neurotransmitters, which are chemicals in the brain that transmit signals between nerve cells. Specifically, imbalances in the neurotransmitters serotonin, dopamine, and norepinephrine have been implicated in the development of the bipolar disorder. Serotonin is a neurotransmitter that is involved in the regulation of mood, sleep, appetite, and other functions. Some studies have suggested that people with bipolar disorder may have lower levels of serotonin during depressive episodes, and higher levels of serotonin during manic or hypomanic episodes. Dopamine is a neurotransmitter that is involved in reward and motivation, as well as movement and coordination. Some research has suggested that abnormalities in the dopamine system may contribute to the development of the bipolar disorder. Norepinephrine is a neurotransmitter that is involved in the body's stress response. Some studies have suggested that people with bipolar disorder may have elevated levels of norepinephrine during manic or hypomanic episodes. While the exact role of neurotransmitter imbalances in bipolar disorder is not yet fully understood, it is believed that medications that affect these neurotransmitters, such as mood stabilizers and antidepressants, can be effective in treating the condition.

3. **Environmental factors**: Trauma, stressful life events, and substance use can all contribute to the onset or exacerbation of bipolar disorder symptoms. Additionally, disruptions in sleep patterns and exposure to seasonal changes or light cycles may also play a role.

In addition to genetics and brain chemistry, environmental factors can also contribute to the development of the bipolar disorder. Some potential environmental factors that have been linked to the condition include:

❖ **Trauma**: Exposure to trauma, such as physical or sexual abuse, can increase the risk of developing bipolar disorder.

❖ Stressful life events: Major life events, such as the loss of a loved one or a job, can trigger the onset of bipolar disorder or exacerbate existing symptoms.

❖ **Substance use**: Substance use, particularly the use of stimulants like cocaine or amphetamines, can trigger manic or hypomanic episodes in individuals with bipolar disorder.

❖ **Sleep disruption**: Disruptions in sleep patterns, such as insomnia or irregular sleep schedules, can trigger or exacerbate bipolar disorder symptoms.

❖ **Seasonal changes**: Some people with bipolar disorder may experience seasonal changes in their mood, with depressive episodes occurring more frequently in the winter months.

While these environmental factors can increase the risk of developing bipolar disorder, not everyone who experiences them will develop the condition. Additionally, other factors, such as genetics and brain chemistry, can also play a role in the development of the bipolar disorder.

4. **Neurological factors**: Neurological factors are another potential contributor to the development of the bipolar disorder. Studies have suggested that people with bipolar disorder may have structural and functional differences in certain areas of the brain compared to people without the condition. Some specific neurological factors that have been linked to the bipolar disorder include:

❖ Abnormalities in the prefrontal cortex: The prefrontal cortex is a region of the brain involved in decision-making, impulse control, and emotional regulation. Some studies have suggested that people with bipolar disorder may have abnormalities in the prefrontal cortex that contribute to the development of the condition.

❖ Changes in the size and activity of the amygdala: The amygdala is a region of the brain involved in emotional processing. Some studies have suggested that people with bipolar disorder may have changes in the size and activity of the amygdala that contribute to mood instability.

❖ Alterations in white matter: White matter refers to the fibers that connect different regions of the brain. Some studies have suggested that people with bipolar disorder may have alterations in white matter that contribute to the development of the condition.

❖ It's important to note that while neurological factors may play a role in the development of the bipolar disorder, it is likely that multiple factors, including genetics, brain chemistry, and environmental factors, interact to contribute to the condition.

The Categories Of Bipolar Disorder

Bipolar disorder is categorized into several types, based on the pattern and severity of symptoms experienced by the individual. The categories of bipolar disorder include:

1. **Bipolar I disorder**: This type of bipolar disorder involves the presence of at least one manic episode that lasts for at least one week (or requires hospitalization). Individuals with bipolar I disorder may also experience depressive episodes.
2. **Bipolar II disorder:** This type of bipolar disorder involves the presence of at least one major depressive episode and at least one hypomanic episode (a less severe form of mania that lasts for at least four days). Individuals with bipolar II disorder do not experience full-blown manic episodes.
3. **Cyclothymic disorder**: This type of bipolar disorder involves the presence of numerous periods of hypomanic and depressive symptoms that do not meet the criteria for a full-blown manic or depressive episode. These symptoms must be present for at least two years (or one year in children and adolescents).
4. **Other specified and unspecified bipolar and related disorders:** This category includes bipolar-like conditions that do not meet the full diagnostic criteria for bipolar I, bipolar II, or cyclothymic disorder. Examples include brief periods of manic symptoms or depressive symptoms that do not meet the duration criteria for a full episode.

It's important to note that the specific type of bipolar disorder diagnosed can impact the course of treatment and management strategies recommended by healthcare professionals.

Bipolar I Disorder

Bipolar I disorder is the most severe form of bipolar disorder and is characterized by the presence of at least one manic episode. A manic episode is a period of elevated or irritable mood, as well as increased energy or activity levels. During a manic episode, an individual may experience:

- Grandiosity or inflated self-esteem
- Decreased need for sleep
- Racing thoughts
- Increased talkativeness
- Impulsivity or recklessness (such as engaging in risky behaviors like spending sprees, drug use, or sexual indiscretions)
- Psychotic symptoms (such as delusions or hallucinations)

A manic episode must last for at least one week (or require hospitalization), and must cause significant impairment in social, occupational, or other areas of functioning. In some cases, individuals with bipolar I disorder may also experience depressive episodes, which involve symptoms such as sadness, loss of interest or pleasure in activities, changes in appetite or sleep, and feelings of worthlessness or guilt.

Bipolar I disorder can be a highly debilitating condition, and can significantly impact an individual's ability to function in day-to-day life. Treatment typically involves a combination of medication and psychotherapy and may include mood stabilizers, antipsychotic medications, antidepressants, or other medications as needed. It's important for individuals with bipolar I disorder to receive ongoing treatment and support in order to manage their symptoms and improve their quality of life.

Bipolar II Disorder

Bipolar II disorder is a type of bipolar disorder that involves the presence of at least one major depressive episode and at least one hypomanic episode, which is a less severe form of mania than experienced in bipolar I disorder. The symptoms of hypomania are similar to those experienced during a manic episode, but are less severe and do not involve psychosis or significant impairment in functioning.

During a hypomanic episode, an individual may experience:
- Increased energy or activity levels
- Racing thoughts
- Increased talkativeness
- Impulsivity or recklessness
- Grandiosity or inflated self-esteem

The hypomanic episode must last for at least four days, and must be different from the individual's usual mood and behavior. In contrast to bipolar I disorder, individuals with bipolar II disorder do not experience full-blown manic episodes.

The depressive episodes experienced by individuals with bipolar II disorder are similar to those experienced in other types of depression, and may include symptoms such as sadness, loss of interest or pleasure in activities, changes in appetite or sleep, and feelings of worthlessness or guilt.

Bipolar II disorder can still be a significant challenge for individuals who experience it, and may impact their ability to function in daily life. Treatment typically involves a combination of medication and psychotherapy, and may include mood stabilizers, antipsychotic medications, antidepressants, or other medications as needed. It's important for individuals with bipolar II disorder to receive ongoing treatment and support in order to manage their symptoms and improve their quality of life.

Cyclothymic Disorder

Cyclothymic disorder is a type of bipolar disorder that involves the presence of numerous periods of hypomanic and depressive symptoms that do not meet the criteria for a full-blown manic or depressive episode. The symptoms of the cyclothymic disorder are less severe than those experienced in bipolar I or II disorder, but they are still persistent and disruptive to daily functioning.

During a hypomanic period, an individual with the cyclothymic disorder may experience symptoms such as:

- Increased energy or activity levels
- Racing thoughts
- Increased talkativeness
- Impulsivity or recklessness
- Grandiosity or inflated self-esteem

During a depressive period, an individual with the cyclothymic disorder may experience symptoms such as:

- Sadness or hopelessness
- Loss of interest or pleasure in activities
- Changes in appetite or sleep
- Fatigue or loss of energy
- Feelings of worthlessness or guilt

The symptoms of cyclothymic disorder must be present for at least two years (or one year in children and adolescents), with no more than two symptom-free months in a row during that time. Individuals with the cyclothymic disorder may experience periods of stability or mild symptoms, but their mood swings can still impact their daily life.

Treatment for the cyclothymic disorder may involve a combination of medication and psychotherapy, including mood stabilizers, antidepressants, or other medications as needed. Psychotherapy, such as cognitive-behavioral therapy or interpersonal therapy, can also be helpful in managing symptoms and improving quality of life. It's important for individuals with cyclothymic disorder to receive ongoing treatment and support in order to manage their symptoms and improve their overall functioning.

SCHIZOAFFECTIVE DISORDER

Schizoaffective disorder is a mental health condition that combines symptoms of both schizophrenia and a mood disorder, such as bipolar disorder or major depressive disorder. The symptoms of schizoaffective disorder can vary greatly between individuals, but typically involve a combination of psychotic symptoms (such as delusions, hallucinations, and disorganized thinking) and mood symptoms (such as depression or mania).

In order to be diagnosed with schizoaffective disorder, an individual must have:

1. Symptoms of schizophrenia, include:
- Delusions (false beliefs that are not based in reality)
- Hallucinations (sensory experiences that are not based in reality)
- Disorganized thinking or speech
- Abnormal behaviors or movements
2. Symptoms of a mood disorder, include:

- Major depressive episodes, which involve persistent sadness or loss of interest in activities, along with symptoms such as changes in appetite or sleep, fatigue, and feelings of worthlessness or guilt
- Manic or hypomanic episodes, which involve elevated or irritable mood, increased energy or activity levels, and other symptoms similar to those experienced in bipolar disorder

The symptoms of schizoaffective disorder can be highly disruptive to an individual's daily life and may require ongoing treatment and support. Treatment for the schizoaffective disorder may involve a combination of medication and psychotherapy, including antipsychotic medications, mood stabilizers, antidepressants, or other medications as needed. Psychotherapy, such as cognitive-behavioral therapy or family therapy, can also be helpful in managing symptoms and improving quality of life. It's important for individuals with schizoaffective disorder to receive ongoing treatment and support in order to manage their symptoms and improve their overall functioning.

THE MANIA PHASE

Mania is a state of elevated, expansive, or irritable mood that is one of the defining features of bipolar disorder. During a manic episode, an individual may experience a range of symptoms that can significantly impact their daily functioning and overall well-being.

Symptoms of the manic phase of bipolar disorder may include:
- **Elevated or irritable mood:** During a manic episode, an individual may feel euphoric, extremely happy, or unusually irritable, or agitated. They may feel like

they have endless energy and may engage in excessive talking or talk faster than usual.

- **<u>Increased energy and activity levels</u>:** Mania is often characterized by a sudden increase in energy, leading to a feeling of restlessness and a need to keep moving. This may manifest as excessive pacing or fidgeting, as well as engaging in impulsive behaviors such as spending sprees, reckless driving, or substance use.
- **<u>Reduced need for sleep</u>:** During a manic episode, an individual may require less sleep than usual, and may feel fully rested after just a few hours of sleep.
- **<u>Racing thoughts</u>:** Mania can also involve a heightened sense of creativity and productivity, but it can also lead to rapid, racing thoughts that are difficult to control. These thoughts may be disconnected or unrelated, making it difficult for the individual to focus or concentrate.
- **<u>Impulsive or risky behaviors</u>:** During a manic episode, individuals may engage in impulsive or risky behaviors, such as unprotected sex, substance abuse, or reckless spending.
- **<u>Grandiosity or inflated self-esteem</u>:** Mania may also involve feelings of grandiosity, such as believing that one has special abilities, talents, or powers. This may manifest as believing one is invincible, or that they have a special relationship with a celebrity, deity, or another prominent figure.

If left untreated, the manic phase of bipolar disorder can escalate into a state of psychosis, which involves a loss of touch with reality and can be very dangerous. It's important for individuals experiencing symptoms of mania to seek professional help in order to manage their symptoms and reduce the risk of harm to themselves or others. Treatment may include medication, psychotherapy, or a combination of both.

The Depression Phase

Depression is a mood disorder characterized by persistent feelings of sadness, hopelessness, and lack of interest in activities that used to bring pleasure. It can affect how a person thinks, feels, and behaves, and can significantly impact their daily functioning, including their ability to work, study, and maintain relationships.

Depression can occur in different forms, including major depressive disorder, dysthymia, seasonal affective disorder, and postpartum depression. Symptoms can vary from person to person, but common symptoms may include:

- **Persistent sadness or feelings of emptiness**: Individuals with depression may experience a persistently low mood that lasts for weeks or months. They may feel empty, hopeless, or worthless, and may lose interest in activities that they once enjoyed.
- **Loss of energy or fatigue**: Depression can also cause a significant decrease in energy levels, making even simple tasks feel overwhelming or exhausting.
- **Changes in appetite or sleep**: Depression can also affect an individual's appetite and sleep patterns. Some people with depression may experience increased appetite and weight gain, while others may lose their appetite and experience weight loss. Similarly, some individuals may experience insomnia, while others may sleep excessively.
- **Difficulty concentrating or making decisions**: Depression can make it difficult to focus or

concentrate, and can affect an individual's ability to make decisions or complete tasks.

- **Feelings of guilt or worthlessness**: Depression can also involve feelings of guilt or worthlessness, leading individuals to blame themselves for their condition or feel undeserving of help or support.
- **Suicidal thoughts or behaviors:** In some cases, depression can lead to thoughts of suicide or self-harm. Individuals experiencing suicidal thoughts or behaviors should seek immediate professional help.

Chapter Two

Navigating a Bipolar Diagnosis

Getting A Proper Diagnosis

Getting a proper diagnosis of depression is important for receiving appropriate treatment and managing symptoms effectively. Here are some steps you can take to get a proper diagnosis:

1. **Schedule an appointment with a mental health professional**: The first step is to make an appointment with a mental health professional, such as a psychologist or psychiatrist, who can evaluate your symptoms and provide a diagnosis.

2. **Be open and honest about your symptoms**: It's important to be honest with your mental health professional about your symptoms, even if they are difficult to talk about. This can help ensure that you receive an accurate diagnosis and appropriate treatment.

3. **Provide a complete medical history:** Your mental health professional may ask about your medical history, including any previous mental health issues, medications you're taking, and any other health conditions you may have.

4. **Undergo a mental health evaluation**: Your mental health professional may conduct a mental health evaluation, which can involve questions about your symptoms, medical history, and any other relevant information. This can help determine whether you meet the diagnostic criteria for depression.

5. **Consider getting a second opinion**: If you're unsure about your diagnosis or treatment plan, consider getting a second opinion from another mental health professional.

Remember, depression is a treatable condition, and getting a proper diagnosis is the first step towards managing your symptoms and improving your quality of life. Don't be afraid to seek help if you're experiencing symptoms of depression.

Common Challenges Of A Bipolar Diagnosis

Receiving a bipolar disorder diagnosis can be a challenging experience for many individuals. Here are some common challenges that people may face after receiving a bipolar disorder diagnosis:

Stigma

Stigma and discrimination are major challenges faced by individuals with bipolar disorder. Stigma refers to the negative attitudes and beliefs that society holds towards mental illness, which can lead to prejudice, discrimination, and social exclusion.

Stigma can manifest in different ways, such as:

1. **Stereotyping:** People with bipolar disorder may be stereotyped as "crazy," "unstable," or "violent," which can be hurtful and inaccurate.

2. **Blame and shame**: People with bipolar disorder may be blamed for their condition or made to feel ashamed of their symptoms, which can lead to feelings of isolation and low self-esteem.

3. **Misunderstanding:** There may be a lack of understanding about the nature of the bipolar disorder, leading to misconceptions and fear.

Discrimination can occur in different areas of life, such as employment, education, housing, and healthcare. Discrimination can include being denied opportunities, experiencing negative treatment, and having access to fewer resources.

The stigma and discrimination associated with bipolar disorder can have serious consequences for individuals, including:

1. **Delayed or inadequate treatment**: Stigma and discrimination can prevent individuals from seeking or receiving proper treatment for their condition.
2. **Social isolation**: Stigma and discrimination can lead to social isolation and exclusion, which can negatively impact mental health.
3. **Lowered self-esteem**: Negative attitudes towards bipolar disorder can lead to lowered self-esteem and a negative self-image.

It's important to challenge stigma and discrimination by raising awareness, educating others, and promoting acceptance and understanding of mental illness. This can help individuals with bipolar disorder feel more supported and included in society, and can ultimately improve mental health outcomes.

Difficulty accepting a diagnosis of bipolar disorder

Difficulty accepting a diagnosis of bipolar disorder is a common challenge that many individuals face. It can be overwhelming and scary to receive a diagnosis of a mental illness, and it's not uncommon for people to experience a range of emotions such as denial, shock, anger, and sadness. Some reasons why individuals may have difficulty accepting the diagnosis of bipolar disorder can include:

1. **Fear of stigma and discrimination**: As mentioned earlier, there is still a significant stigma attached to mental illness, and people may fear being judged or discriminated against due to their diagnosis.
2. **Lack of understanding**: Individuals may have limited knowledge or understanding of the bipolar disorder, leading to confusion or disbelief about their diagnosis.
3. **Loss of identity**: Receiving a bipolar disorder diagnosis can sometimes cause people to feel like they have lost a sense of who they are or that their diagnosis defines them.
4. **Worry about medication**: Some people may be hesitant to start taking medication for bipolar disorder due to concerns about side effects or the stigma associated with medication for mental illness.
5. **Hopelessness**: Receiving a bipolar disorder diagnosis can sometimes lead to feelings of hopelessness and despair, particularly if the individual has been struggling with their symptoms for some time.

Relationship Issues

Relationship issues are a common challenge for individuals with bipolar disorder and their loved ones. Bipolar disorder can impact many areas of a person's life, including their relationships with family, friends, and romantic partners.

Some challenges that may arise in relationships due to bipolar disorder can include:

1. **Communication difficulties**: Bipolar disorder can cause changes in mood and behavior, which can lead to difficulty communicating effectively with loved ones.

2. **Unpredictable behavior**: The unpredictable nature of the bipolar disorder can make it challenging for loved ones to know how to respond or provide support.

3. **Mood swings:** Bipolar disorder can cause mood swings, which can be difficult for loved ones to navigate and understand.

4. **Irritability or aggression**: In some cases, bipolar disorder can cause irritability or aggression, which can negatively impact relationships.

5. **Lack of intimacy**: Bipolar disorder can sometimes lead to a decrease in intimacy or a lack of interest in sexual activity, which can cause strain on romantic relationships.

6. **Caregiver burden**: For family members or partners who provide support and care for someone with bipolar disorder, the role can be emotionally and physically demanding, which can lead to caregiver burden and stress.

It's important for individuals with bipolar disorder and their loved ones to work together to address relationship issues and find ways to manage symptoms. This can include seeking therapy, attending support groups, practicing healthy communication, and developing coping strategies. With time and effort, it's possible to build strong and supportive relationships while managing the challenges of bipolar disorder.

Medication Side Effects

Medication side effects are another common challenge that individuals with bipolar disorder may face. Many medications used to treat bipolar disorder can cause side effects, which can range from mild to severe. Some common side effects of bipolar disorder medication can include:

1. **Weight gain**: Many medications used to treat bipolar disorder can cause weight gain, which can be distressing for some individuals.
2. **Sleep disturbances**: Some medications used to treat bipolar disorder can cause sleep disturbances, such as insomnia or excessive sleepiness.
3. **Nausea and digestive problems**: Some people may experience nausea, vomiting, or other digestive problems when taking bipolar disorder medication.
4. **Sexual dysfunction**: Some medications used to treat bipolar disorder can cause sexual dysfunction, such as a decrease in libido or difficulty achieving orgasm.
5. **Tremors:** Some people may experience tremors or shaking when taking bipolar disorder medication.
6. **Cognitive problems**: Some medications used to treat bipolar disorder can cause cognitive problems, such as difficulty concentrating or memory problems.

It's important to discuss any side effects with a healthcare provider to determine if they are temporary or if they require an adjustment to the medication dosage or a change in medication. In some cases, the benefits of the medication may outweigh the side effects. However, in other cases, a healthcare provider may recommend trying a different medication to manage symptoms while minimizing side effects.

Difficulty managing symptoms

Difficulty managing symptoms is a common challenge for individuals with bipolar disorder. Symptoms of bipolar disorder can be disruptive and make it difficult to manage daily life activities such as work, school, or social interactions. Some common symptoms of bipolar disorder include:

1. **Mood swings**: Bipolar disorder can cause extreme shifts in mood, which can be difficult to manage.
2. **Irritability or agitation**: Some people with bipolar disorder may experience irritability or agitation, which can make it difficult to interact with others.
3. **Fatigue or low energy**: Depression, a common symptom of bipolar disorder, can cause fatigue or low energy levels, making it challenging to complete daily activities.
4. **Racing thoughts or difficulty concentrating**: Some people with bipolar disorder may experience racing thoughts or difficulty concentrating, which can make it challenging to focus on tasks.
5. **Impulsivity:** Bipolar disorder can cause impulsivity, which can lead to risky behaviors or decisions.

Financial Challenges

Financial challenges can be another common issue for individuals with bipolar disorder. Bipolar disorder can affect a person's ability to work and maintain financial stability, which can lead to financial stress and hardship. Some common financial challenges that individuals with bipolar disorder may face include:

1. **Unemployment or underemployment**: Symptoms of bipolar disorder can make it difficult to maintain employment or work consistently, which can lead to financial instability.
2. **Medical expenses**: The cost of medical care, including medication and therapy, can be expensive and may not always be covered by insurance.
3. **Impulsivity**: Bipolar disorder can cause impulsivity, which can lead to impulsive spending or risky financial decisions.
4. **Debt**: Individuals with bipolar disorder may struggle with managing finances and may accumulate debt as a result.
5. **Legal issues**: In some cases, individuals with bipolar disorder may face legal issues, such as bankruptcy or foreclosure, as a result of financial instability.

Stigma Surrounding Bipolar Disorder

Stigma surrounding bipolar disorder refers to negative attitudes, beliefs, and stereotypes that are associated with the disorder. Stigma can be a major barrier to individuals seeking treatment and can impact their ability to manage their condition effectively. Some common examples of stigma surrounding bipolar disorder include:

1. **Misconceptions about the disorder**: Many people have misconceptions about bipolar disorder, such as the belief that individuals with the disorder are violent or unstable.
2. **Blaming the individual**: Some individuals may be blamed for their condition or told that they simply need to "snap out of it," which can be hurtful and dismissive of the challenges they face.
3. **Discrimination:** Individuals with bipolar disorder may face discrimination in various areas of life, such as employment, housing, or social relationships.
4. **Self-stigma**: Individuals with bipolar disorder may internalize negative attitudes and beliefs about their condition, which can lead to feelings of shame and self-blame.

Stigma can be harmful and can prevent individuals from seeking the treatment and support they need. It's important to challenge stigma and promote understanding and acceptance of bipolar disorder. Some strategies for challenging stigma include:

1. **Educating others**: Providing accurate information about bipolar disorder can help to dispel misconceptions and reduce stigma.
2. **Speaking out**: Sharing personal stories and experiences can help to reduce stigma by humanizing the disorder and challenging negative stereotypes.
3. **Advocating for change**: Advocacy efforts can help to change policies and practices that contribute to stigma and discrimination.
4. **Promoting acceptance**: Encouraging acceptance and understanding of individuals with bipolar disorder can help to create a more inclusive and supportive society.

It's important to recognize that stigma surrounding bipolar disorder is a real and significant challenge, but by working together to challenge stigma and promote understanding, we can create a more accepting and supportive world for individuals with bipolar disorder.

Coping Strategies For Managing A Bipolar Diagnosis

Seeking Professional Help

Seeking professional help is an important step in managing bipolar disorder. A mental health professional, such as a psychiatrist, psychologist, or clinical social worker, can provide diagnosis, treatment, and ongoing support.

When seeking professional help, it's important to find a mental health professional who has experience and expertise in treating bipolar disorder. Some ways to find a qualified mental health professional include:

1. Referrals from a primary care physician or another healthcare provider.
2. Referrals from family, friends, or support groups.
3. Searching online for mental health professionals in your area who specialize in bipolar disorder.
4. Contacting your insurance company to see which mental health professionals are covered by your insurance plan.

Once you have found a mental health professional, it's important to schedule an appointment and discuss your symptoms and concerns. Your mental health professional will likely conduct an evaluation, which may include a clinical interview, a medical exam, and psychological testing, to determine if you have bipolar disorder or another mental health condition.

If you are diagnosed with bipolar disorder, your mental health professional can work with you to develop a treatment plan that may include medication, therapy, and lifestyle changes. It's important to follow your treatment plan and attend all scheduled appointments to get the best results from treatment.

Remember, seeking professional help is a sign of strength, and it can be an important step in managing bipolar disorder and improving the overall quality of life.

Medication Management

Medication management is an important part of treating bipolar disorder. Medications can help to stabilize mood, reduce symptoms, and prevent relapse. There are several types of medications that may be used to treat bipolar disorder, including mood stabilizers, antipsychotics, and antidepressants.

Mood stabilizers, such as lithium, valproate, and carbamazepine, are often used to treat bipolar disorder. These medications can help to reduce the severity and frequency of mood swings and can help to prevent relapse. Antipsychotic medications, such as risperidone, olanzapine, and quetiapine, may also be used to treat bipolar disorder. These medications can help to reduce symptoms of mania and psychosis.

Antidepressants may also be used to treat bipolar disorder, but they are often used in combination with a mood stabilizer or antipsychotic medication. Antidepressants can help to reduce symptoms of depression, but they can also trigger manic or hypomanic episodes in some people with bipolar disorder.

It's important to work closely with a healthcare provider to find the right medication and dosage for you. Medication management may require regular check-ins with a healthcare provider to monitor symptoms and adjust medication as needed.

It's also important to be aware of the potential side effects of medication and to report any side effects to your healthcare provider. Some common side effects of bipolar medications include weight gain, drowsiness, dizziness, and tremors. In some cases, medication may need to be adjusted or changed to manage side effects.

Remember, medication is just one part of treating bipolar disorder. It's also important to engage in other forms of treatment, such as therapy and lifestyle changes, to manage symptoms and improve the overall quality of life.

Self-care

Self-care is an important part of managing bipolar disorder. It involves taking care of your physical, emotional, and mental health through various strategies and practices. Here are some self-care strategies that may be helpful for people with bipolar disorder:

1. **Get enough sleep:** Sleep is important for regulating mood and reducing symptoms of bipolar disorder. Try to establish a regular sleep routine and aim for 7-9 hours of sleep each night.

2. **Eat a healthy diet:** Eating a balanced diet with plenty of fruits, vegetables, and whole grains can help to improve overall health and well-being.
3. **Exercise regularly:** Regular exercise can help to reduce symptoms of depression and anxiety, improve mood, and promote overall health.
4. **Practice stress-management techniques**: Stress can trigger mood swings in people with bipolar disorder. Engage in stress-management techniques such as meditation, deep breathing, or yoga to help manage stress.
5. **Avoid alcohol and drugs**: Alcohol and drugs can interfere with medication and trigger mood swings in people with bipolar disorder. Avoid using these substances to promote stability and well-being.
6. **Build a support system:** Having a support system of family, friends, or a support group can help to reduce feelings of isolation and provide emotional support.
7. **Practice good self-care habits**: Engage in activities that promote relaxation, such as taking a warm bath, reading a book, or practicing a hobby that you enjoy.

Remember, self-care is an ongoing process and it may take some time to find strategies that work best for you. It's important to be patient and consistent in practicing self-care to help manage symptoms and promote overall health and well-being.

Stress Reduction

Stress reduction is an important aspect of managing bipolar disorder, as stress can trigger mood swings and exacerbate symptoms. Here are some stress reduction strategies that may be helpful:

1. **Identify sources of stress**: Identify the situations or people that cause you to stress, so you can develop a plan to manage them.
2. **Practice relaxation techniques**: Engage in relaxation techniques such as deep breathing, progressive muscle relaxation, or yoga to help reduce stress and promote relaxation.
3. **Exercise regularly**: Exercise is a great way to reduce stress and improve overall physical and mental health. Aim for at least 30 minutes of exercise most days of the week.
4. **Maintain a healthy lifestyle**: Eating a healthy diet, getting enough sleep, and avoiding alcohol and drugs can help to reduce stress and promote overall well-being.
5. **Prioritize self-care**: Set aside time for activities that you enjoy and that help you to relax and unwind, such as reading, taking a bath, or spending time in nature.
6. **Seek support:** Talk to a therapist or join a support group to get help managing stress and developing coping strategies.

Remember, stress reduction is an ongoing process and it may take some time to find strategies that work best for you. It's important to be patient and consistent in practicing stress reduction techniques to help manage symptoms and promote overall health and well-being.

Psychotherapy, also known as talk therapy, can be a helpful treatment for managing bipolar disorder. There are several types of psychotherapy that may be beneficial for people with bipolar disorder, including:

1. **Cognitive-behavioral therapy (CBT):** CBT helps people with bipolar disorder to identify and change negative thought patterns and behaviors that can trigger mood swings.

2. **Interpersonal and social rhythm therapy (IPSRT):** IPSRT focuses on establishing regular routines and reducing stressful life events, which can help to regulate mood.

3. **Family-focused therapy**: This type of therapy involves family members in treatment and helps them to understand bipolar disorder and provide support to their loved ones.

4. **Supportive therapy**: Supportive therapy involves talking to a therapist about the challenges of living with bipolar disorder and receiving emotional support.

Psychotherapy can be used alone or in combination with medication to manage bipolar disorder. It's important to work with a qualified mental health professional who has experience in treating bipolar disorder and to be open and honest about your experiences and needs in therapy.

Education And Self-Awareness

Education and self-awareness are important components of managing bipolar disorder. Learning about the disorder can help individuals understand their symptoms, recognize triggers, and develop coping strategies. Some ways to increase education and self-awareness include:

1. **Research**: Educate yourself about bipolar disorder by reading books, articles, and reputable online resources.
2. **Attend support groups**: Joining a support group can provide an opportunity to learn from others who are experiencing similar challenges.
3. **Track symptoms**: Keep a mood journal to track mood swings, sleep patterns, and other symptoms. This can help identify triggers and patterns.
4. **Learn stress management techniques:** Learning stress management techniques such as deep breathing, mindfulness, and meditation can help reduce the impact of stress on mood.
5. **Communication**: Communicate openly and honestly with your healthcare provider, family, and friends about your experiences and needs.
6. **Self-care**: Prioritize self-care and practice healthy habits such as regular exercise, healthy eating, and adequate sleep.

By increasing education and self-awareness, individuals with bipolar disorder can take an active role in managing their symptoms and achieving a better quality of life.

Finding The Right Treatment Plan

Finding the right treatment plan for bipolar disorder can take time and may involve trial and error. Here are some tips for finding the right treatment plan:

1. **Consult with a mental health professional**: A mental health professional can help diagnose bipolar disorder and develop an individualized treatment plan.

2. **Consider medication options**: Medications such as mood stabilizers, antipsychotics, and antidepressants may be prescribed to manage symptoms of bipolar disorder. It's important to work closely with a healthcare provider to find the right medication and dosage that works best for you.

3. **Explore therapy options**: Psychotherapy can be a helpful adjunct to medication in managing bipolar disorder. Different types of therapy, such as cognitive-behavioral therapy or interpersonal therapy, may be recommended based on an individual's needs.

4. **Consider lifestyle changes**: Lifestyle changes such as regular exercise, healthy eating habits, and stress management techniques can also be beneficial in managing bipolar disorder.

5. **Collaborate with healthcare providers**: It's important to have open communication with healthcare providers to ensure that the treatment plan is effective and any concerns or side effects are addressed.

6. **Be patient:** Finding the right treatment plan may take time and require adjustments along the way. It's important to be patient and persistent in working towards managing bipolar disorder effectively.

Ultimately, finding the right treatment plan requires a personalized approach that takes into account an individual's unique needs and experiences. By working with healthcare providers and exploring different treatment options, individuals with bipolar disorder can find a plan that works best for them.

CHAPTER THREE

The Treatment Of Bipolar Disorder

Medication is often a cornerstone of treatment for bipolar disorder. There are several classes of medications that can be effective in treating bipolar disorder, including mood stabilizers, antipsychotics, and antidepressants. Lithium, a mood stabilizer, is often considered the gold standard in the treatment of the bipolar disorder, as it has been shown to reduce the frequency and severity of manic and depressive episodes. Other mood stabilizers commonly used include valproic acid, carbamazepine, and lamotrigine. Antipsychotics may be used to treat acute manic or mixed episodes, and some may also have mood-stabilizing properties. Antidepressants are generally not used alone in the treatment of the bipolar disorder, as they can trigger manic or hypomanic episodes.

Psychotherapy, or talk therapy, can also be an important component of treatment for bipolar disorder. Cognitive behavioral therapy (CBT) is often used to help individuals with bipolar disorder identify and change negative thought patterns and behaviors that may contribute to their symptoms. Interpersonal and social rhythm therapy (IPSRT) can help individuals with bipolar disorder establish and maintain a regular routine, which can be important in preventing mood episodes. Family-focused therapy (FFT) involves working with individuals with bipolar disorder and their family members to improve communication, reduce stress, and enhance problem-solving skills.

Lifestyle changes can also be helpful in managing bipolar disorder. These may include maintaining a regular sleep schedule, eating a healthy diet, exercising regularly, avoiding alcohol and drugs, and reducing stress. In addition, individuals with bipolar disorder should work with their healthcare provider to develop a crisis plan, which outlines steps to take if they experience a mood episode.

Overall, the treatment of bipolar disorder should be individualized to meet the specific needs of each individual. It is important for individuals with bipolar disorder to work closely with their healthcare providers to develop a comprehensive treatment plan that addresses their unique symptoms and challenges.

Lithium

Lithium is a naturally occurring element that has been used as a medication for bipolar disorder since the 1950s. Lithium is often considered the gold standard treatment for bipolar disorder, as it has been shown to be effective in reducing the frequency and severity of manic and depressive episodes.

Lithium works by affecting the balance of certain chemicals in the brain, particularly those involved in the regulation of mood and behavior. It is thought to enhance the activity of certain neurotransmitters, such as serotonin, and to reduce the activity of others, such as dopamine.

One of the benefits of lithium is that it can be effective in treating both manic and depressive episodes, and can help to prevent future episodes from occurring. However, it can take several weeks for lithium to take effect, and it must be carefully monitored to ensure that the dosage is correct and that there are no adverse side effects.

Common side effects of lithium include tremors, increased thirst and urination, weight gain, and nausea. In rare cases, lithium can cause more serious side effects, such as kidney or thyroid problems, so regular blood tests are necessary to monitor for these issues.

Overall, lithium can be a highly effective treatment for bipolar disorder, but it requires careful monitoring and management to ensure that it is safe and effective for each individual.

Exploring the powerful impact of lithium in preventing suicide in individuals with bipolar disorder

Lithium is a medication that has been used for over 50 years to treat bipolar disorder, and numerous studies have shown that it can significantly reduce the risk of suicide and suicide attempts in individuals with this condition.

Research has shown that lithium works by stabilizing mood and reducing the severity and frequency of manic and depressive episodes. In addition to its mood-stabilizing properties, lithium also has a unique anti-suicide effect that is not seen with other mood stabilizers or antidepressant medications. Studies have found that lithium can reduce the risk of suicide attempts by as much as 80% in people with bipolar disorder.

Despite its effectiveness, lithium is not without its drawbacks. It requires careful monitoring to ensure that blood levels remain within a therapeutic range, and some people may experience side effects such as tremors, weight gain, and thirst. However, for many people with bipolar disorder, the benefits of lithium in reducing the risk of suicide and stabilizing mood outweigh the potential risks.

It is important to note that lithium is not the only treatment option for bipolar disorder and that other medications and therapies may be more appropriate for some individuals. It is important for individuals with bipolar disorder to work closely with their healthcare providers to develop a comprehensive treatment plan that meets their individual needs and preferences.

Lithium Toxicity

Lithium toxicity is a potentially serious condition that occurs when there is too much lithium in the body. It can result from an overdose of lithium medication or from normal doses that accumulate in the body over time.

Lithium toxicity can have serious effects on the body, including affecting the central nervous system, kidneys, and cardiovascular system. In severe cases, it can lead to coma or death. The symptoms of lithium toxicity can include confusion

- tremors
- drowsiness
- slurred speech
- vomiting
- diarrhea
- seizures.

It is important to seek medical attention immediately if these symptoms occur, especially if the individual is taking lithium as a medication for bipolar disorder.

If symptoms of lithium toxicity are present, treatment should be sought immediately. Treatment may involve stopping lithium medication, administering fluids and electrolytes, and in severe cases, hemodialysis. It is important for individuals taking lithium to be aware of the signs and symptoms of toxicity and to report them to their healthcare provider promptly.

Lithium Blood Tests

Lithium blood tests are tests that measure the level of lithium in the blood. They are commonly used to:
- Monitor lithium levels during treatment to ensure they are within a therapeutic range
- Adjust the dose of lithium as needed
- Monitor for potential toxicity
- Identify any potential drug interactions
- Determine if a person is taking their prescribed dose of lithium

The test involves taking a blood sample from the arm, which is then sent to a laboratory for analysis. The results of the test can help inform treatment decisions and ensure that lithium is being used safely and effectively. It is important for individuals taking lithium to have regular blood tests as directed by their healthcare provider.

Antipsychotics

Antipsychotics are a class of medications used primarily to treat psychotic disorders such as schizophrenia and bipolar disorder. They work by blocking the activity of dopamine, a neurotransmitter that is involved in the regulation of mood, emotions, and perceptions. Antipsychotics are also used to treat other conditions such as severe anxiety, depression, and obsessive-compulsive disorder. There are two main types of antipsychotics: typical (or first-generation) antipsychotics and atypical (or second-generation) antipsychotics. Atypical antipsychotics are newer medications that have been developed to be more effective and have fewer side effects than typical antipsychotics.

Some common atypical antipsychotics used to treat bipolar disorder include:

- Aripiprazole (Abilify)
- Olanzapine (Zyprexa)
- Quetiapine (Seroquel)
- Risperidone (Risperdal)
- Ziprasidone (Geodon)

These medications are generally used in conjunction with other treatments, such as mood stabilizers, to help manage symptoms of bipolar disorder. They can be particularly helpful in treating manic episodes, as they can help to reduce agitation, irritability, and other symptoms associated with mania.

As with all medications, atypical antipsychotics can have side effects, and it is important to work closely with a healthcare provider to monitor symptoms and adjust treatment as needed. Some common side effects of atypical antipsychotics include

- weight gain
- drowsiness
- dizziness
- increased risk of diabetes
- high cholesterol.

Brain Stimulation Treatments

Brain stimulation treatments are non-invasive or minimally invasive procedures that involve the use of electrical or magnetic energy to stimulate specific regions of the brain. These treatments are typically used for individuals who have not responded well to other treatments for bipolar disorder or who experience severe symptoms that are difficult to manage. There are several types of brain stimulation treatments, including:

Electroconvulsive Therapy (ECT)

Electroconvulsive therapy (ECT) is a brain stimulation treatment that involves passing electric currents through the brain to induce a controlled seizure. It is primarily used to treat severe depression, mania, and psychosis that is unresponsive to other treatments. ECT is usually administered under general anesthesia and involves placing electrodes on the scalp to deliver the electric currents. The exact mechanism of action of ECT is not fully understood, but it is thought to alter the levels of neurotransmitters in the brain and affect neural connectivity. ECT is generally considered safe but can cause side effects such as headaches, muscle soreness, and confusion. It is typically used as a last resort when other treatments have not been effective.

Transcranial magnetic stimulation (TMS)

Transcranial magnetic stimulation (TMS) is a non-invasive brain stimulation technique that uses a magnetic field to stimulate nerve cells in the brain. It is typically used as a treatment for depression that has not responded to other forms of therapy, although it has also been investigated for the treatment of the bipolar disorder.

During a TMS session, the patient sits in a chair and a coil is placed on their scalp. The coil produces a magnetic field that stimulates nerve cells in the brain. The treatment is usually given daily for several weeks.

TMS is generally considered safe, with few serious side effects. However, some patients may experience headaches, scalp discomfort, or other mild side effects. It is important to note that TMS is not appropriate for everyone and should only be used under the guidance of a qualified healthcare professional.

Vagus Nerve Stimulation (VNS)

Vagus nerve stimulation (VNS) is a type of brain stimulation therapy that involves implanting a device that sends electrical impulses to the vagus nerve, which is located in the neck. The vagus nerve is a major nerve in the body that connects the brain to various organs, including the heart, lungs, and digestive system. By stimulating the vagus nerve, VNS can help regulate certain brain functions and improve mood and symptoms of depression or epilepsy.

During VNS therapy, a small device called a pulse generator is surgically implanted under the skin in the chest. The pulse generator is connected to the vagus nerve by a thin wire that runs under the skin. The device sends electrical impulses to the vagus nerve at regular intervals, typically several times a day.

VNS therapy has been approved by the FDA for the treatment of epilepsy and depression but has not responded to other treatments. It may also be used off-label to treat other conditions, such as bipolar disorder.

As with any medical treatment, VNS therapy may have side effects, which can include hoarseness, coughing, and shortness of breath. In rare cases, VNS therapy may cause more serious side effects, such as infection or nerve damage.

Antidepressants

Antidepressants are medications used to treat depression and other mental health conditions such as anxiety, obsessive-compulsive disorder, and post-traumatic stress disorder. They work by increasing the levels of certain neurotransmitters in the brain, such as serotonin, norepinephrine, and dopamine, which are believed to be involved in regulating mood.

There are several different types of antidepressants, including selective serotonin reuptake inhibitors (SSRIs), serotonin-norepinephrine reuptake inhibitors (SNRIs), tricyclic antidepressants (TCAs), and monoamine oxidase inhibitors (MAOIs). Each type works in a slightly different way, and some may be more effective for certain people or conditions than others.

Like all medications, antidepressants can have side effects. Common side effects include nausea, dizziness, insomnia, and sexual dysfunction. In some cases, they can also increase the risk of suicidal thoughts or behavior, especially in children, teenagers, and young adults.

Antidepressants are usually prescribed by a mental health professional, such as a psychiatrist or a primary care doctor. It is important to follow the prescribed dosage and to report any side effects to the prescribing doctor. In some cases, a combination of antidepressants and other medications may be recommended for optimal treatment. Psychotherapy and other non-medication treatments may also be recommended in conjunction with medication.

Communication Strategies

Effective communication refers to the ability to express your thoughts, feelings, and needs clearly and respectfully, while also actively listening to your partner's perspective. Effective communication is essential in managing the challenges of bipolar disorder, as it allows both partners to understand each other's needs, feelings, and experiences, and work together to find solutions to problems. Effective communication also involves using specific techniques such as active listening, using "I" statements, avoiding judgment and blame, being respectful, and using nonverbal communication to convey empathy and understanding. Overall, effective communication is a critical component of building a strong and healthy relationship when one partner has bipolar disorder.

Importance Of Open Communication

Open communication is crucial when it comes to managing bipolar disorder. Here are some reasons why:

1. Promotes understanding: Open communication can help individuals with bipolar disorder and their loved ones better understand the condition, its symptoms, and its impact on daily life.

2. Encourages seeking help: Talking openly about bipolar disorder can reduce stigma and encourage individuals to seek professional help when needed.

3. Facilitates treatment: Open communication with healthcare providers can help ensure that the right treatment plan is developed and that any concerns or side effects are addressed.

4. Strengthens relationships: Open communication can help strengthen relationships and build trust between individuals with bipolar disorder and their loved ones.

5. Reduces conflict: Misunderstandings and unspoken concerns can lead to conflict in relationships. Open communication can help address these issues and prevent conflicts from arising.

6. Promotes self-awareness: Talking openly about bipolar disorder can help individuals become more aware of their symptoms, triggers, and needs, which can aid in managing the condition effectively.

Overall, open communication is essential for individuals with bipolar disorder and their loved ones to effectively manage the condition and promote overall well-being.

Effective Communication Techniques

Effective communication is key when it comes to managing bipolar disorder. Here are some techniques that can help:

Active listening

Active listening is a communication technique that involves giving full attention to the person speaking, understanding what they are saying, and responding appropriately. Here are some tips for active listening:

1. **Pay attention**: When someone is speaking, give them your full attention. Avoid distractions such as looking at your phone or thinking about other things.
2. **Show that you are listening**: Use nonverbal cues, such as nodding your head or making eye contact, to show that you are paying attention and interested in what the other person is saying.
3. **Clarify:** If you are unsure about what the person is saying, ask for clarification. Repeat back what you heard and ask if you understood correctly.
4. **Summarize:** After the person has finished speaking, summarize what you heard to make sure you understood correctly. This can also help the other person feel heard and understood.
5. **Respond appropriately**: Respond in a way that shows you are engaged in the conversation and have heard what the other person has said. This can include asking follow-up questions, offering your own perspective, or simply acknowledging their feelings.

Active listening can help improve communication and build stronger relationships. It shows that you are interested in what the other person has to say and can help prevent misunderstandings.

Using "I" statements

Using "I" statements is a communication technique that involves expressing your thoughts, feelings, and needs using the pronoun "I" rather than "you." This can help to avoid blame and defensiveness in a conversation and promote more effective communication. Here are some examples of how to use "I" statements:

- Instead of saying "You never listen to me," try saying "I feel ignored when I talk and it makes me upset."
- Instead of saying "You are always late," try saying "I get anxious when people are late and it would be helpful for me if we could stick to the agreed-upon schedule."
- Instead of saying "You are being unreasonable," try saying "I have a different perspective on this and I would like to discuss it more so we can understand each other better."

By using "I" statements, you are taking responsibility for your own feelings and needs, rather than placing blame on the other person. This can make the other person more open to hearing what you have to say and can promote more effective communication and problem-solving.

Avoiding judgment

Avoiding judgment is a communication technique that involves refraining from criticizing or evaluating the other person or their actions, beliefs, or feelings. This can help to create a safe and non-threatening environment for communication and prevent defensiveness and misunderstandings. Here are some tips for avoiding judgment:

1. **Practice empathy**: Try to put yourself in the other person's shoes and understand their perspective, feelings, and needs without judging or criticizing.
2. **Use neutral language**: Use neutral or non-judgmental language when expressing your thoughts or feelings. For example, instead of saying "That's a terrible idea," you could say "I have some concerns about that approach."
3. **Focus on the behavior, not the person:** When discussing a problem or issue, focus on the specific behavior or action that you want to address, rather than criticizing the person. For example, instead of saying "You are lazy," you could say "I noticed that the task is not completed, can you tell me more about what happened?"
4. **Ask open-ended questions**: Ask open-ended questions that encourage the other person to share their thoughts and feelings without feeling judged or criticized. For example, instead of saying "Why did you do that?", you could say "Can you tell me more about what led you to make that decision?"

By avoiding judgment, you can create an environment that promotes open communication and problem-solving. This can help to build trust and understanding in relationships and lead to more positive outcomes.

Being clear and concise

Being clear and concise is an effective communication technique that involves expressing your thoughts and feelings in a clear and straightforward manner. Here are some tips for being clear and concise in your communication:

1. **Use simple language**: Use simple and easy-to-understand language when expressing your thoughts or feelings.
2. **Avoid jargon or technical terms**: Avoid using jargon or technical terms that the other person may not be familiar with, as this can cause confusion and misunderstandings.
3. **Stay focused**: Stay focused on the main point or message that you want to convey, and avoid going off on tangents or getting sidetracked.
4. **Be specific**: Use specific examples or details to support your message and help the other person understand what you are saying.
5. **Use active voice**: Use active voice instead of passive voice when expressing your thoughts or feelings. For example, instead of saying "Mistakes were made," say "I made a mistake."

By being clear and concise in your communication, you can help to ensure that your message is understood and prevent misunderstandings or confusion. This can promote effective problem-solving and lead to more positive outcomes in relationships.

Being Respectful

Being respectful is an important aspect of effective communication. When communicating with someone, it is important to treat them with respect and consideration, regardless of whether you agree with their opinions or not. Here are some ways to show respect in communication:

1. **Listen actively**: Listening actively and attentively to what the other person is saying shows that you value their thoughts and feelings.
2. **Avoid interrupting**: Interrupting someone while they are speaking can be disrespectful and prevent them from fully expressing themselves.
3. **Use polite language**: Using polite language, such as "please" and "thank you," can help to convey respect and consideration.
4. **Avoid using offensive language**: Avoid using offensive language, including derogatory terms or slurs, as this can be hurtful and disrespectful.
5. **Acknowledge differences**: Recognize and acknowledge that everyone has different opinions and perspectives, and show respect for these differences.

By being respectful in your communication, you can build trust and foster positive relationships with others. This can also help to reduce conflicts and promote effective problem-solving.

Using nonverbal communication

Nonverbal communication can be just as important as verbal communication when it comes to effectively communicating with others. Here are some ways to use nonverbal communication to enhance your communication:

1. **Maintain eye contact**: Maintaining eye contact with the other person can show that you are interested in what they are saying and that you are actively listening.

2. **Use facial expressions**: Your facial expressions can convey emotions and help to reinforce what you are saying. For example, a smile can convey friendliness, while a frown can indicate displeasure.

3. **Use body language**: Your body languages, such as your posture and gestures, can also convey meaning and emotion. For example, crossing your arms may indicate defensiveness, while leaning forward may show interest.

4. **Use the tone of voice: The** tone of your voice can also convey emotions and meaning. For example, speaking in a calm and even tone can convey a sense of reassurance while speaking in a raised and rapid tone may indicate anger or frustration.

5. **Pay attention to the other person's nonverbal cues:** Just as your nonverbal communication can convey meaning, so can the other person's. Pay attention to their body language, facial expressions, and tone of voice to better understand their feelings and intentions.

Using nonverbal communication can help to enhance your verbal communication and make it more effective. By paying attention to your own nonverbal cues and those of the other person, you can better understand their thoughts and feelings and improve the overall quality of your communication.

Strategies For Handling Conflict

Conflict is a natural part of any relationship, but it can be particularly challenging when one or both partners have bipolar disorder. Here are some strategies for handling conflict:

1. **Take a break**: If the conflict is getting heated, take a break and come back to the conversation when you're both feeling calmer.
2. **Use "I" statements**: When expressing your perspective, use "I" statements to avoid sounding accusatory or critical. For example, say "I feel hurt when you do X" instead of "You always do X and it's so frustrating."
3. **Avoid blame**: Try to avoid blaming your partner for the conflict. Instead, focus on finding solutions and moving forward.
4. **Listen actively**: When your partner is speaking, focus on what they are saying and try to understand their perspective. Avoid interrupting or getting defensive.
5. Find common ground: Look for areas of agreement and work together to find solutions that meet both partners' needs.
6. **Use humor:** Humor can be a great way to diffuse tension and lighten the mood. However, be careful not to use humor in a way that minimizes or dismisses your partner's feelings.

7. **<u>Seek outside help</u>**: If you're having trouble resolving conflicts on your own, consider seeking outside help from a therapist or couples counselor.

Remember that conflict is a normal part of any relationship, and it's important to approach it with a spirit of collaboration and respect. By using these strategies, you can improve the quality of your communication and build a stronger relationship with your partner.

CHAPTER FOUR

Supporting Your Partner Through Bipolar Disorder

Supporting a partner with bipolar disorder can be challenging, and it is essential to have a strong support network in place. Here are some strategies for building a support network:

1. **Reach out to family and friends**: Reach out to trusted family and friends who can offer support and understanding. They can help you navigate the challenges of bipolar disorder and provide a listening ear when you need to talk.

2. **Seek support groups**: Support groups can be a valuable resource for both you and your partner. They offer a safe space to share experiences and connect with others who are going through similar challenges.

3. **Connect with mental health professionals**: Mental health professionals such as therapists and psychiatrists can provide guidance and support in managing bipolar disorder. They can offer coping strategies, medication management, and other resources to support you and your partner.

4. **Consider couple's therapy:** Couple's therapy can be a useful tool for improving communication, strengthening your relationship, and managing the challenges of bipolar disorder together.

5. **Take care of yourself**: Remember to prioritize self-care and take care of your own mental health needs. This can include engaging in activities you enjoy,

getting enough sleep, and seeking support when needed.

By building a strong support network, you and your partner can navigate the challenges of bipolar disorder together and find the support and resources you need to maintain a healthy relationship.

Managing The Ups And Downs Of Bipolar Disorder

Managing the ups and downs of bipolar disorder can be challenging, but there are several strategies that can help. Here are some tips for managing the highs and lows of bipolar disorder:

Create a daily routine

Creating a daily routine can be helpful in managing the ups and downs of bipolar disorder. This routine should include regular sleep patterns, exercise, healthy eating habits, and medication schedules. Having a consistent routine can help stabilize mood and reduce the risk of triggering manic or depressive episodes.

Some tips for creating a daily routine include:

1. **Set a regular sleep schedule**: Go to bed and wake up at the same time each day, even on weekends.
2. **Incorporate exercise**: Regular exercise can help stabilize mood, reduce stress, and improve overall health. Aim for at least 30 minutes of exercise each day.
3. **Plan healthy meals**: Eating a balanced diet can help regulate mood and energy levels. Plan meals and

snacks that include a variety of fruits, vegetables, whole grains, and lean proteins.

4. **Take medication as prescribed**: Follow medication schedules as prescribed by a healthcare professional. Do not adjust the dosage or stop taking the medication without consulting a healthcare professional.

5. **Incorporate relaxation techniques**: Practices such as mindfulness, deep breathing, and yoga can help reduce stress and anxiety.

6. **Schedule regular activities**: Engage in activities that are enjoyable and promote a sense of purpose, such as hobbies, social activities, and volunteering.

Remember that everyone's daily routine will be different, and it may take some trial and error to find a routine that works well for you or your loved one with bipolar disorder.

Monitor symptoms

Monitoring symptoms is an important aspect of managing bipolar disorder. It involves keeping track of mood changes, sleep patterns, and other symptoms, such as anxiety or irritability. By monitoring symptoms, individuals and their loved ones can identify patterns and triggers, and adjust treatment plans accordingly.

Some ways to monitor symptoms include keeping a journal or mood chart, using a mood-tracking app, or working with a healthcare provider to develop a personalized monitoring plan. It's important to regularly review symptoms with a healthcare provider and adjust treatment plans as needed.

Example of a mood-tracking app

There are several mood-tracking apps available for smartphones that can help individuals with bipolar disorder monitor their symptoms. Here are a few examples:

1. **Daylio**: This app allows users to track their moods, activities, and habits. It also offers the ability to set reminders and track progress over time.

2. **Moodfit:** This app includes mood tracking, daily journaling, and a symptom checker. It also offers guided meditation and relaxation exercises.

3. **eMoods:** This app allows users to track their mood, sleep, medications, and other symptoms. It also includes a customizable report generator to share with healthcare providers.

4. **MoodTracker**: This app allows users to track their mood, anxiety, and other symptoms. It also includes a customizable reminder system and the ability to export data to share with healthcare providers.

It's important to note that while these apps can be helpful tools for monitoring symptoms, they should not replace the advice and guidance of a healthcare provider.

Practice stress-reduction techniques

Stress can be a significant trigger for individuals with bipolar disorder, so it's important to practice stress-reduction techniques to help manage symptoms. Here are some strategies that can be helpful:

1. **Mindfulness meditation**: Mindfulness meditation involves paying attention to the present moment without judgment. This practice has been shown to reduce stress and improve overall well-being.

2. **Exercise**: Regular exercise can help reduce stress and improve mood. It can also help with sleep and overall physical health.
3. **Relaxation techniques**: Techniques such as deep breathing, progressive muscle relaxation, and visualization can help reduce stress and promote relaxation.
4. **Time management**: Managing time effectively can reduce stress and help individuals feel more in control of their daily routines. This might involve setting priorities, breaking tasks into manageable pieces, and setting realistic goals.
5. **Social support**: Spending time with supportive friends and family members can help reduce stress and improve mood. Joining a support group can also provide a valuable source of support and understanding.

It's important to note that everyone's stress-reduction needs and preferences are different, so it may be helpful to experiment with different techniques to find what works best for you.

Get enough sleep

Getting enough sleep is crucial for managing bipolar disorder as it can help regulate mood and prevent episodes of mania or depression. People with bipolar disorder may find it challenging to maintain a regular sleep schedule, but there are several strategies that can help:

1. **Stick to a consistent sleep schedule**: Try to go to bed and wake up at the same time every day, even on weekends.
2. **Create a sleep-conducive environment**: Make sure your bedroom is dark, quiet, and cool. Invest in comfortable bedding and a supportive mattress.
3. **Wind down before bedtime**: Develop a relaxing bedtime routine, such as taking a warm bath or reading a book.
4. **Limit caffeine and alcohol**: These substances can interfere with sleep and trigger mood episodes.
5. **Talk to your doctor about sleep medications**: If you're having trouble sleeping, your doctor may be able to prescribe medication to help.

By prioritizing sleep and developing healthy sleep habits, people with bipolar disorder can better manage their symptoms and improve their overall quality of life.

Be aware of medication side effects

Being aware of medication side effects is an important part of managing bipolar disorder. Some medications used to treat bipolar disorder can have side effects such as weight gain, fatigue, tremors, or cognitive problems. It's important to talk to your healthcare provider about any side effects you are experiencing so they can adjust your medication or dosage as needed.

In addition to medication side effects, it's important to be aware of any interactions with other medications or substances, including alcohol and recreational drugs. These can affect the effectiveness of your bipolar disorder medication and can also have dangerous interactions.

It's important to work with your healthcare provider to find the right medication and dosage that works for you while minimizing side effects and interactions with other substances. Regular check-ins with your healthcare provider can help monitor and adjust your medication as needed.

Develop a crisis plan

Developing a crisis plan is an important step in supporting a partner with bipolar disorder. The crisis plan should include specific instructions on what to do in case of a bipolar episode, such as a manic or depressive episode, or a medication reaction. It should include contact information for the partner's healthcare providers, emergency contacts, and crisis hotlines.

The crisis plan should also include steps to take to keep the partner safe, such as removing weapons or dangerous objects from the home, and ways to avoid triggering situations. It's important to review and update the crisis plan regularly with the help of the partner's healthcare providers, and to make sure that all members of the support network are aware of the plan and know how to implement it if necessary.

CHAPTER FIVE

Nurturing Your Relationship

Being in a relationship with someone who has bipolar disorder can present both challenges and opportunities. On the one hand, the symptoms of bipolar disorder can cause stress and strain on the relationship. On the other hand, a relationship can provide important support and stability for someone with bipolar disorder.

Some of the challenges that may arise in a relationship with someone with bipolar disorder include:

1. **Mood swings**: The mood swings associated with bipolar disorder can be difficult to predict and manage, and can be especially challenging in a romantic relationship.
2. **Medication side effects**: Some medications used to treat bipolar disorder can cause side effects that may impact the relationship, such as weight gain, fatigue, or sexual dysfunction.
3. **Communication difficulties**: Communication can be a challenge when one partner has bipolar disorder, particularly during times of mania or depression.
4. **Stigma and discrimination**: The stigma surrounding mental illness can make it difficult for couples to share their struggles with others or seek support.

Despite these challenges, there are also opportunities for growth and connection in a relationship with someone with bipolar disorder. For example:

1. **Increased empathy and understanding**: Partners in a relationship with someone with bipolar disorder may develop a greater understanding and empathy for the challenges of living with mental illness.

2. **Stronger communication skills**: Working together to navigate the ups and downs of bipolar disorder can help couples develop stronger communication skills.
3. **A deeper emotional connection**: Going through difficult times together can deepen emotional intimacy and strengthen the bond between partners.

Understanding the impact of bipolar disorder on intimacy

Bipolar disorder can have a significant impact on intimacy in a relationship. During depressive episodes, individuals may experience a lack of energy or motivation and may withdraw emotionally from their partner. This can lead to a feeling of distance or disconnection between partners and can make it difficult to maintain physical intimacy.

During manic episodes, individuals may experience increased energy, impulsivity, and risk-taking behavior. This can lead to a hypersexual state in some individuals, which can be challenging for their partner to navigate. It is important for partners to communicate openly and honestly about their feelings and needs, and to work together to establish healthy boundaries and expectations around intimacy.

It is also important to recognize that bipolar disorder is a chronic condition and that there may be periods of stability as well as periods of mood instability. Partners can work together to navigate these ups and downs, and to find ways to maintain a sense of closeness and intimacy even during difficult times. This may involve finding new ways to connect, such as engaging in shared hobbies or interests or simply spending quality time together.

Building A Fulfilling Future Together

Building a fulfilling future together with a partner who has bipolar disorder can be challenging, but it is possible with the right approach and support. Here are some strategies that can help:

1. **Setting shared goals**: Work with your partner to identify shared goals that you can work towards together. This can help you stay focused on a positive future and give you a sense of purpose.

2. **Focus on the present**: While it's important to have goals for the future, it's also important to focus on the present moment. This means enjoying the time you spend together and being present in the moment.

3. **Engage in enjoyable activities**: Engage in activities that you both enjoy, whether it's going for a walk, seeing a movie, or trying a new restaurant. This can help you stay connected and build positive memories together.

4. **Support your partner's treatment**: Encourage your partner to stick to their treatment plan and offer support and encouragement along the way. This can help them manage their symptoms and stay on track.

5. **Communicate openly**: Open and honest communication is key to building a strong relationship. Make sure to communicate your needs and feelings in a non-judgmental way and listen actively to your partner's perspective.

6. **Seek outside support**: Consider seeking support from a therapist or support group. This can help you both work through any challenges and build a strong foundation for your relationship.

Maintaining a strong emotional connection

Maintaining a strong emotional connection with a partner who has bipolar disorder can be challenging, but it is important for the health of the relationship. Here are some tips for nurturing emotional intimacy:

1. **Practice active listening**: Listen to your partner without judgment and with an open mind. Pay attention to their words, body language, and tone of voice.

2. **Validate your partner's feelings**: Acknowledge your partner's emotions and show empathy. Let them know that their feelings matter to you.

3. **Communicate your own feelings**: Express your own emotions and feelings in a way that your partner can understand. Use "I" statements to avoid blaming or accusing.

4. **Find common ground**: Look for shared interests and activities that you both enjoy. This can help to build a sense of connection and create positive memories.

5. **Celebrate successes together:** Recognize and celebrate your partner's achievements, no matter how small. This can help to boost their self-esteem and create positive momentum.

6. **Be patient and understanding**: Bipolar disorder can be a difficult condition to live with, and your partner may struggle with their emotions and behavior. Practice patience and understanding, and be willing to offer support and assistance when needed.

7. **Seek professional help**: If you are having difficulty maintaining emotional intimacy in your relationship, consider seeking professional help. A therapist or counselor can provide guidance and support to help

you and your partner navigate the challenges of bipolar disorder.

Caring For Yourself

Understanding the importance of self-care

Self-care is the practice of taking actions that promote physical, emotional, and mental well-being. It involves prioritizing your own needs, recognizing your limits, and taking steps to prevent burnout and stress. Self-care is especially important when you are caring for someone with bipolar disorder, as the demands of the relationship can be significant. Taking care of yourself can help you to stay healthy, happy, and engaged in your own life, which in turn can benefit your partner.

There are many different self-care strategies that you can use, including:

1. **Prioritizing your own needs**: This may involve setting aside time each day for activities that you enjoy, such as reading, exercising, or spending time with friends.
2. **Practicing stress-reduction techniques**: This may involve deep breathing exercises, meditation, or yoga.
3. **Getting enough sleep**: Adequate sleep is essential for physical and mental health. Try to establish a consistent sleep routine and avoid caffeine and alcohol before bed.
4. **Seeking support**: This may involve talking to friends or family members, joining a support group, or seeing a therapist.

5. **Engaging in self-reflection**: This may involve journaling, practicing mindfulness, or engaging in other activities that help you to understand and regulate your own emotions.
6. **Setting boundaries**: It is important to set limits on what you are willing and able to do, and to communicate these boundaries clearly to your partner.

By taking care of yourself, you can better support your partner and the relationship as a whole.

Setting Boundaries And Managing Expectations

Setting boundaries and managing expectations is an important aspect of self-care when supporting a partner with bipolar disorder. It is important to recognize and communicate your own needs and limits in the relationship, and to ensure that you are not sacrificing your own well-being for the sake of your partner's needs.

Here are some tips for setting boundaries and managing expectations:

1. **Communicate openly**: Have an open and honest conversation with your partner about your needs, limitations, and expectations. This will help you both understand each other's perspectives and come up with a plan that works for both of you.
2. **Be clear and specific**: When setting boundaries, be clear and specific about what you are comfortable with and what you are not. This will help avoid confusion and ensure that both partners are on the same page.
3. **Stick to your boundaries**: Once you have set your boundaries, it is important to stick to them. This will

help you maintain your own well-being and prevent your partner from unintentionally crossing a line.

4. **Manage expectations**: Recognize that bipolar disorder is a chronic condition that may require ongoing management. Be realistic about what you can and cannot do, and manage your partner's expectations accordingly.

5. **Practice self-care**: Make sure to prioritize your own self-care, including activities that help you relax and recharge. This will help you maintain your own well-being and be a more effective support for your partner.

Finding Your Own Support Network

As a caregiver, it is important to have your own support network to turn to when you need help. Here are some ways to find a support network:

Reach out to friends and family

If you are a caregiver or support person for someone with bipolar disorder, it is important that you also have your own support network. This can help you manage your own stress and avoid burnout.

One way to find support is to reach out to friends and family. They may be able to offer you emotional support, help with practical tasks, or just be someone to talk to. It can be helpful to share your experiences with others who may have gone through similar situations.

You can also consider joining a support group for caregivers of people with bipolar disorder. These groups provide a safe space for you to share your experiences, ask questions, and receive support from others who understand what you are going through.

Additionally, you may benefit from seeking professional help, such as therapy or counseling. A mental health professional can help you develop coping strategies, manage your stress, and address any mental health concerns you may have.

Join a support group

Joining a support group can be a helpful way to connect with others who are going through similar experiences and to find support and understanding. Support groups may be available through local mental health organizations, hospitals, or community centers. There are also online support groups and forums that can provide a sense of community and support, especially for those who may not have access to in-person groups. It is important to find a support group that is a good fit and to participate regularly to get the most benefit.

Seek professional help

Seeking professional help can be an important part of self-care for caregivers of individuals with bipolar disorder. It's important to prioritize your own mental and emotional health, and professional support can help you manage stress and cope with the challenges of caregiving.

You can speak to a therapist, counselor, or mental health professional who has experience working with caregivers of individuals with bipolar disorder. They can offer support, guidance, and coping strategies tailored to your specific needs and circumstances.

Additionally, your loved one's mental health provider may be able to offer guidance and support for caregivers, including referrals to resources such as support groups or educational programs.

Remember, taking care of yourself is essential for your well-being as well as that of your loved one with bipolar disorder. Don't hesitate to reach out for help and support when you need it.

Take care of yourself

Taking care of yourself is essential when you are supporting someone with bipolar disorder. It is essential to maintain your mental and physical health to be able to provide the necessary support to your loved one. Some ways to take care of yourself include:

1. Prioritize self-care activities: Make time for activities that bring you joy and relaxation, such as exercise, reading, or spending time with friends.
2. Practice stress-reduction techniques: Engage in activities that help you manage stress, such as mindfulness meditation, yoga, or deep breathing exercises.
3. Seek support: Reach out to friends, family, or a mental health professional for support and guidance.
4. Set boundaries: It is essential to set boundaries and take care of your needs, as this will help you maintain your physical and mental well-being.
5. Practice self-compassion: Be kind to yourself and acknowledge that caring for a loved one with bipolar disorder can be challenging. Remember that it is okay to make mistakes and that you are doing the best you can.

Remember that taking care of yourself is not selfish but rather an essential component of being an effective caregiver.

CHAPTER SIX

How bipolar disorder can affect long-term plans?

Bipolar disorder can have a significant impact on long-term plans, as it can be unpredictable and disruptive. It may require adjustments to career plans, financial goals, and even family planning. It is important to have open and honest communication with your partner about how the disorder may impact your future plans.

One way to manage the impact of bipolar disorder on long-term plans is to focus on creating a stable and supportive environment. This may involve working with a mental health professional to develop a treatment plan that effectively manages symptoms, as well as implementing self-care strategies and stress-reduction techniques.

It is also important to develop a plan for managing any potential crises that may arise in the future. This may involve creating a crisis plan, identifying support resources, and being prepared to adjust plans as needed in response to the ups and downs of the disorder.

Overall, with the right treatment, support, and planning, it is possible to create a fulfilling and successful future despite the challenges of bipolar disorder.

Building a fulfilling life together

Building a fulfilling life together means creating a life that supports the needs and aspirations of both partners, even in the face of bipolar disorder. It involves communication, compromise, and teamwork to achieve shared goals, while also supporting individual needs and interests.

To build a fulfilling life together, it's important for both partners to identify their values, priorities, and goals. This can involve discussing career aspirations, family planning, and financial goals, among other things. It's also important to be open and honest about the impact of bipolar disorder on these plans and to work together to find ways to manage symptoms and build resilience.

Building a fulfilling life together also involves creating a supportive and nurturing environment. This can involve cultivating shared interests and hobbies, as well as creating routines and traditions that support emotional well-being. It's also important to build a strong network of support, whether it's through friends, family, or a support group.

Ultimately, building a fulfilling life together involves being open to change, adaptation, and growth. It requires a commitment to each other and to the shared goal of creating a life that is fulfilling, rewarding, and resilient in the face of challenges.

Celebrating successes and finding hope

Celebrating successes and finding hope is an essential aspect of living with bipolar disorder. It can be easy to get bogged down by the challenges and setbacks that come with the condition, but it's important to remember that there are many moments of joy and accomplishment that can be celebrated along the way.

One way to celebrate successes is to set achievable goals and milestones, such as completing a specific task or reaching a personal best in a hobby or interest. Celebrate these accomplishments with your partner and take the time to acknowledge the hard work and effort that went into achieving them.

Finding hope is also critical for maintaining a positive outlook on life. This can involve seeking out positive role models who have successfully managed bipolar disorder, participating in support groups or online communities, or engaging in activities that promote a sense of well-being, such as exercise or meditation.

Remember, living with bipolar disorder is a journey, and there will be ups and downs along the way. However, with the right support, coping strategies, and outlook, it is possible to live a fulfilling and meaningful life together.

Resources And Support For Individuals With Bipolar Disorder And Their Loved Ones.

Resources and support for individuals with bipolar disorder and their loved ones.

There are several resources and support options available for individuals with bipolar disorder and their loved ones. Some of them are:

1. **National Alliance on Mental Illness (NAMI)**: NAMI provides education, support, and advocacy for individuals with mental illness and their families. They have local affiliates and support groups across the United States.

2. **Depression and Bipolar Support Alliance (DBSA):** DBSA offers peer-led support groups, educational resources, and advocacy for individuals with mood disorders and their families.

3. **International Bipolar Foundation**: The International Bipolar Foundation provides education and resources on bipolar disorder, including online support groups and webinars.

4. **The Balanced Mind Parent Network**: The Balanced Mind Parent Network provides resources and support for parents of children and teens with bipolar disorder.

5. Mental Health America: Mental Health America offers resources and support for individuals with mental illness and their families, including a helpline and online support groups.

6. **The Substance Abuse and Mental Health Services Administration (SAMHSA)**: SAMHSA provides a national helpline for individuals and families seeking mental health and substance abuse information and referrals.

7. **Your healthcare provider**: Your healthcare provider can provide information and referrals to local resources and support groups, as well as offer treatment and medication management for bipolar disorder.

It's important to remember that seeking support and treatment for bipolar disorder can make a significant difference in managing symptoms and improving quality of life.

Conclusion

In conclusion, loving someone with bipolar disorder can be challenging, but it can also be immensely rewarding. Building and maintaining a strong relationship requires understanding, patience, and communication. It is important to remember that bipolar disorder is a treatable condition, and with proper management and support, individuals with bipolar disorder can lead fulfilling lives.

Through education, self-care, and a strong support network, caregivers can navigate the ups and downs of bipolar disorder and help their loved ones thrive. By setting boundaries, managing expectations, and seeking professional help when needed, caregivers can avoid burnout and maintain their own mental and emotional well-being.

Most importantly, it is crucial to remember that bipolar disorder does not define a person and that individuals with bipolar disorder are capable of achieving their goals and living meaningful lives. With love, understanding, and support, caregivers can help their loved one with bipolar disorder reach their full potential and enjoy a fulfilling life.

50 Positive Affirmations For Someone With Bipolar Disorder

1. I am worthy of love and respect.
2. I am not defined by my diagnosis.
3. I am capable of managing my symptoms.
4. I am in control of my thoughts and emotions.
5. I choose to focus on the present moment.
6. I am grateful for my support system.
7. I am strong and resilient.
8. I have the power to overcome challenges.
9. I am learning and growing every day.
10. I am proud of myself for seeking help.
11. I deserve to live a fulfilling life.
12. I am surrounded by positivity and light.
13. I am at peace with my past and hopeful for my future.
14. I am patient with myself and my progress.
15. I am mindful of my thoughts and behaviors.
16. I am kind and compassionate towards myself and others.
17. I am capable of achieving my goals and dreams.
18. I am worthy of self-care and self-love.
19. I trust the journey and have faith in myself.
20. I am grateful for every new day and its opportunities.
21. I am deserving of happiness and joy.
22. I am proud of my accomplishments, big and small.
23. I have the ability to cope with stress and anxiety.
24. I am constantly improving my mental health.
25. I am surrounded by love and support.
26. I have the power to overcome any obstacle.
27. I am grateful for my inner strength and resilience.

28. I am committed to my recovery and well-being.
29. I am patient and gentle with myself during difficult times.
30. I am capable of finding peace and calm within myself.
31. I am surrounded by positive energy and light.
32. I am grateful for the lessons that bipolar disorder has taught me.
33. I am open to healing and transformation.
34. I am worthy of forgiveness, both from myself and others.
35. I am committed to self-improvement and growth.
36. I am constantly learning and evolving as a person.
37. I am at peace with my emotions and thoughts.
38. I have the strength to overcome any challenge that comes my way.
39. I am capable of finding happiness and contentment in my life.
40. I am in control of my own happiness and well-being.
41. I am surrounded by positivity and good vibes.
42. I am deserving of love, happiness, and success.
43. I am capable of achieving anything I set my mind to.
44. I am proud of the progress I have made so far.
45. I am worthy of self-care and self-love.
46. I am grateful for the support of my loved ones.
47. I am capable of overcoming my fears and doubts.
48. I am deserving of compassion and understanding.
49. I am constantly growing and evolving as a person.
50. I am at peace with myself and the world around me.

Made in United States
North Haven, CT
12 October 2025

80725148R00049